FUNdamental
Science

Key Stage 1

# Let's Investigate
# Plastic
# Pollution

## On Land and in the Oceans

by Ruth Owen

**With thanks to**
Dr. Laura Foster
Head of Clean Seas
Marine Conservation Society

RUby TUesday BOOKS

Published in 2018 by Ruby Tuesday Books Ltd.

Editor: Mark J. Sachner
Designer: Emma Randall
Production: John Lingham

Photo credits:
Alamy: 20 (bottom), 22 (top), 27 (bottom); Cosmographics: 17 (top); Evoware: 29 (top right), 29 (centre); FLPA: 21, 30–31; Getty Images: 26; Istock Photo: 23 (bottom); Nature Picture Library: 5 (top), 11 (top); OceanwideImages/Gary Bell: 16 (top); Ruby Tuesday Books: 13, 14, 18; Shutterstock: Cover, 1–2, 4, 5 (bottom), 6–7, 8–9, 10, 11 (bottom), 12, 15, 17 (bottom), 19, 20 (top), 22 (bottom), 23 (top), 24–25, 27 (top), 28, 29 (top left), 31 (bottom); Skipping Rocks Lab: 29 (bottom); WashedAshore.org: 30 (bottom).

British Library Cataloguing in Publication Data (CIP) is available for this title.

ISBN 978-1-78856-022-1

Printed in Poland by L&C Printing Group

www.rubytuesdaybooks.com

# Contents

Words shown in **bold** in the text are explained in the glossary.

The download button shows there are free worksheets or other resources available. Go to:

**www.rubytuesdaybooks.com/scienceKS1**

# A Plastic Problem

We all use plastic every day. Some plastic objects make our lives safer or more fun.

Plastic helmet

Plastic football

Plastic net

But sometimes plastic is used to make things we don't actually need.

The BIG problem with plastic is that when people throw it away, it doesn't disappear.

In fact, almost every piece of plastic that's ever been made is still on Earth somewhere.

When plastic is thrown away, it often ends up in the ocean.

Seal pups playing with plastic

Up to 13 million tonnes of plastic enters the world's oceans each year. That's the same as a dumper truck of rubbish every minute of every day!

Scientists estimate that 9 out of 10 seabirds have plastic in their stomachs.

It's time to solve the problem of plastic **pollution** and everyone can help!

# What Is Plastic?

Plastic is a material that's produced in factories. It is made from oil, coal, gas, **chemicals** and other materials.

Plastic objects can be made in any shape or colour.

A polyester football shirt

Some fabrics, such as polyester, are made from plastics.

Nurdles

These tiny beads are pellets of plastic, known as **nurdles**. In factories, the pellets are heated and melted. Then the melted plastic can be shaped into different objects.

6

Plastic can be used to make long-lasting parts for computers, cars and planes.

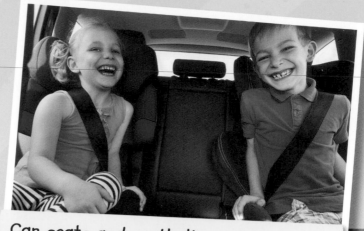

Car seats and seatbelts contain plastic.

It can even be used to make plastic bones for people who have been badly injured.

However, not all plastic objects are made to be used again and again.

Let's Talk

What kinds of plastic objects do you think might only be used for a short time?

# Single-Use Plastic

Many plastic objects are made to be used once and then thrown away. They are called single-use plastics.

Shampoo bottle

Cotton buds

Plastic bag

Ketchup sachet

Straws

Cling film

SHAMPOO BOTTLE

Plastic, or polystyrene, box

Some single-use plastics may only be used for a few minutes!

Plastic balloon and string

Water bottle

Plastic cutlery

Cup

Crisp packet

Many single-use plastics are used to package food and drink.

Foods such as potatoes and apples have protective skins. However, many shops sell these foods wrapped in plastic that has to be thrown away.

## Let's Talk

Why do you think some shops sell potatoes and apples packaged in single-use plastic?

## Let's Explore!

Check out the plastic in your home or classroom.

*Can you find the following plastic objects?*

- *3 things that are made to be used again and again.*
- *3 things that are single use and will soon be thrown away.*

# Why Is Plastic a Problem?

A piece of single-use plastic is sometimes used for just a few hours. But after it's thrown away, it may be around forever!

If you bury an apple in the ground it **biodegrades**, or rots away, in a few months.

A biodegrading apple

If you bury a plastic bottle in the ground, it doesn't biodegrade.

In time, a plastic bottle may crack and crumble, but it will still exist as tiny pieces.

Most of the plastic we throw away is still out there somewhere, polluting our world!

Plastic bottles on the seabed

# Be a Scientist!

**Let's investigate how materials biodegrade in soil.**

**Gather your equipment:**
- An apple core
- A small piece of cardboard
- A small piece of thin plastic
- A small trowel
- 3 large pebbles
- A waterproof marker pen
- A small patch of garden soil
- A notebook and pen

1. Write the words Apple, Cardboard and Plastic on the three pebbles with the marker.

2. Dig three small holes about 10 cm deep in the soil and put one material in each.

3. Fill in the holes and place a pebble on top to mark the spot. Leave the materials buried for four weeks.

*How do you think each material will look after four weeks? Record your predictions in your notebook.*

4. After four weeks dig up your materials.

*Did your predictions match what happened?*

If you wish, you can bury your materials again to see what happens next.

(At the end of the experiment, dig up the plastic and **recycle** it or throw it away.)

# Plastics in Landfill

When people throw away plastic it can end up in **landfill**.

A landfill is a big hole in the ground where rubbish is buried.

Many wild animals visit landfills to find food. Sometimes they get tangled in plastic rubbish. They may even eat plastic, thinking it's food.

# What Happens at a Landfill?

Trucks collect rubbish and take it to a landfill.

The rubbish is buried in the ground.

Thick plastic sheets are laid in the hole to stop the rubbish polluting the soil.

Layers of soil

In a landfill plastics and other kinds of rubbish release chemicals that mix with rainwater.

If the protective plastic sheets in the hole split, **toxic** liquids can soak into the soil.

Then this pollution may trickle under the ground and flow into streams, rivers and the ocean.

Let's Talk

How do you think plastic that's thrown away ends up in the ocean?

13

# Plastic in the Ocean

Billions of plastic objects are polluting our oceans. How did they get there?

## A Plastic Bottle's Journey

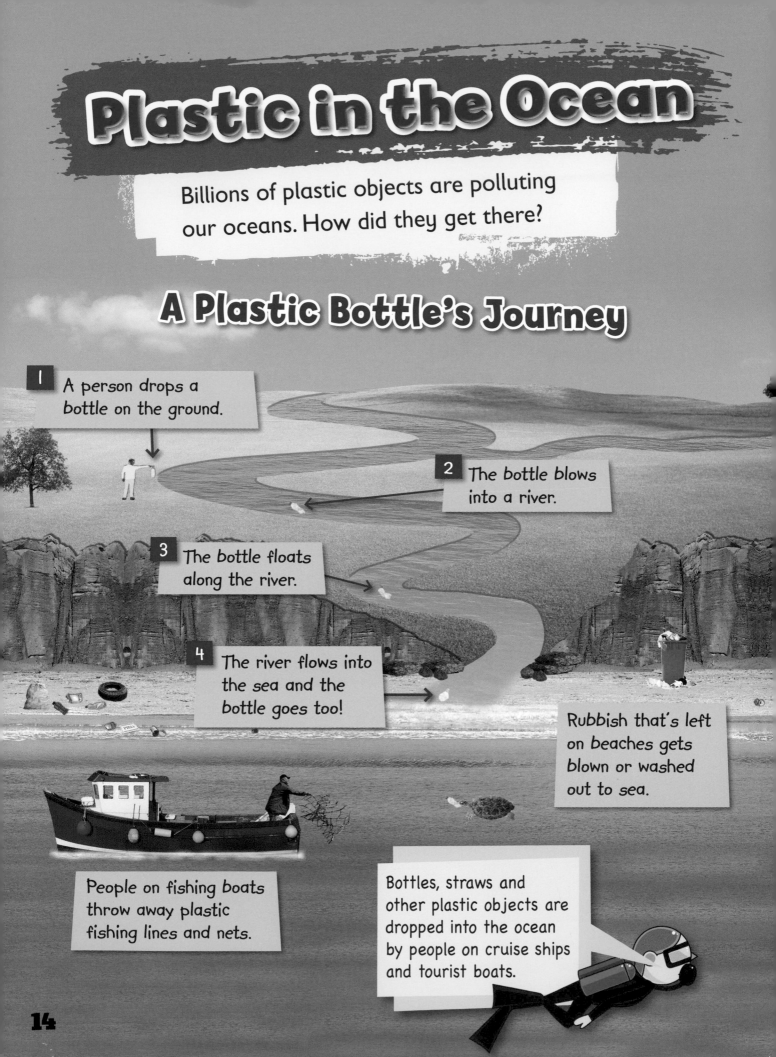

**1** A person drops a bottle on the ground.

**2** The bottle blows into a river.

**3** The bottle floats along the river.

**4** The river flows into the sea and the bottle goes too!

Rubbish that's left on beaches gets blown or washed out to sea.

People on fishing boats throw away plastic fishing lines and nets.

Bottles, straws and other plastic objects are dropped into the ocean by people on cruise ships and tourist boats.

Plastic rubbish that's dropped in the street may get washed down a drain with rainwater.

The drain leads to a river that will eventually flow into the ocean.

Drain

Sometimes, plastic from landfills gets blown into rivers or out to sea.

Things that are flushed down the toilet, such as wet wipes, may end up in the sea. Wet wipes should never be flushed away! They can block **sewers** and many types contain plastic.

Wet wipe

Plastic packaging

Let's Talk

Only three things should be put down the toilet. They all begin with P. What are they?

(The answer is at the bottom of the page.)

**Answer:** Only poo, poo and paper should be flushed down the toilet.

15

# On the Move!

A piece of plastic in the ocean may travel thousands of miles. It is carried by movements of water called **currents**.

This is a beach on one of the Cocos Keeling Islands in the Indian Ocean. No one lives here, but the beach is covered with millions of pieces of plastic.

Ocean currents carry rubbish to the Cocos Keeling Islands from countries far away.

Ocean currents also carry plastic into huge areas of circling water called gyres.

The plastic gets trapped and forms a giant floating rubbish, or garbage, patch.

The Great Pacific Garbage Patch is the biggest.

This world map shows the five main garbage patches.

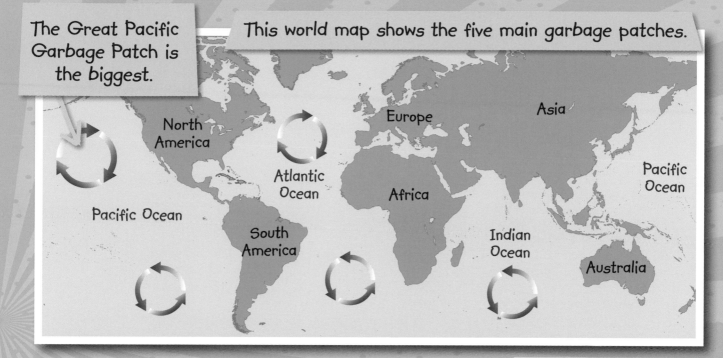

North America

Atlantic Ocean

Pacific Ocean

South America

Europe

Africa

Asia

Indian Ocean

Pacific Ocean

Australia

The water in a garbage patch contains big plastic objects and trillions of tiny pieces of plastic.

Scientists estimate that the plastic in the Great Pacific Garbage Patch weighs the same as 500 jumbo jets!

Let's Talk

Where do you think the tiny pieces of plastic in the ocean come from?

Plastic from a garbage patch

# Microplastics

Once a plastic bottle is in the ocean, the seawater and sunlight make the plastic **brittle**.

The bottle starts to **degrade**.

It crumbles into pieces that become smaller ...

... and smaller ...

... and smaller.

These tiny pieces are called **microplastics**.

Scientists think it will take about 450 years for a plastic bottle to degrade in the ocean.

Seabirds, crabs, squid, fish and other animals may think microplastics are food and eat them.

# Let's Investigate!

Tiny pieces of plastic such as nurdles, microbeads and glitter are also microplastics.

**Nurdles**     **Microbeads in _skin scrubs_**     **Glitter**

*How do you think these microplastics end up in the ocean?*

(The answers are at the bottom of the page.)

Plastic may contain toxic chemicals. Scientists have also discovered that microplastics soak up chemicals that are already in the sea. All these poisons go into an animal's body when it eats microplastics.

# A Plastic Ocean Food Chain

When animals eat microplastics, they might also take in toxic chemicals. This pollution may then be passed up the food chain!

A person eats tuna.

A big fish, such as a tuna, eats the small fish.

Small fish eat microplastics.

Microplastics

**Answers:** Nurdles get washed down drains in factories or spill from ships during transport. Microbeads in skin scrubs and pieces of glitter get washed down the plughole, go through the sewers and end up in the ocean.

# Animals in Danger

Thousands of ocean animals are hurt and killed by plastic pollution every day!

Animals eat rubbish, thinking it's food.

Their stomachs get clogged with plastic.

Then they can't eat real food and they starve to death.

This plastic bag looks like a jellyfish to a turtle.

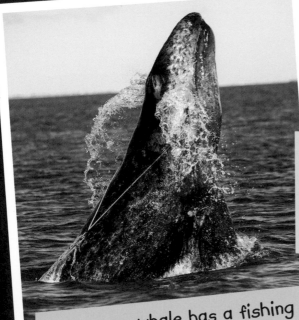

This young whale has a fishing line tangled in its mouth.

Animals may struggle to swim if they get tangled in fishing lines and nets. A whale will drown if it can't swim to the surface to breathe.

**An albatross family**

Sometimes seabirds, such as albatrosses, feed plastic to their chicks. The parent birds think the plastic is food. A chick's stomach gets filled with plastic and it dies.

Scientists collected all this plastic from the stomachs of dead albatross chicks.

**Let's Talk**

What do you think we can do to STOP plastic pollution?

# Let's Recycle It

Many plastic items don't have to be thrown away. They can be recycled.

At a recycling plant, plastic bottles are washed and shredded.

A plastics recycling plant

Crushed plastic bottles

The shredded plastic is melted and turned into nurdles.

Shredded plastic bottles

The nurdles are made into new plastic things.

Unfortunately, many kinds of single-use plastic aren't recycled.

Cling film

Plastic bag

If plastic is combined with another material, it can be difficult and expensive to recycle it.

LIQUID SOAP
Dispenser Pump Bottle

COSMETIC

The top of this soap bottle can't be recycled because it contains metal.

Even recycled plastic can end up in landfill. A plastic bottle may be recycled as stuffing for a sofa. But once the sofa falls apart, it will be thrown away.

Recycling is a great way to stop lots of plastic becoming pollution.

But using less plastic is the best idea of all!

23

# Plastic Free

No matter how good we all get at recycling, we still use too much plastic. It's time to find ways to go plastic free.

Fruits and vegetables don't need to be wrapped in plastic.

Food for sale at a bulk store

At bulk stores people fill up their own long-lasting, reusable containers with food.

# Plastic-Free Things I Can Do Today!

Feeling thirsty? Fill a glass with water from a tap or use a drinking fountain.

Carry a reusable water bottle when you're out and about.

Say NO to plastic straws!

These straws washed up on a beach.

Remind a grown-up to put leftovers into a reusable container instead of wrapping them in cling film.

If you're choosing a gift for an adult, buy them a reusable shopping bag or coffee cup.

Use a bar of soap instead of bottled soap.

If a shop gives you a plastic bag, try to reuse it as many times as possible.

If you help out with shopping, make plastic-free choices. Glass containers are better than plastic because glass can be recycled again and again.

Use a flannel instead of a wet wipe.

# Clean Up the Ocean

Around the world, many people take part in beach clean-ups. Every piece of plastic that's collected is one less piece in the ocean.

The plastic that's collected from beaches can often be recycled.

Scientists try to work out where the rubbish on a beach came from. If they discover a company has dumped rubbish in the sea, the company can be made to stop!

## Let's Investigate!

Imagine you are a scientist at a beach clean-up. Carefully observe all the rubbish in the picture on page 27.

*How many different plastic objects can you spot? Make a list.*

*Choose one object. How do you think it ended up in the ocean? Draw a picture that shows its journey from being used to being in the sea.*

Some beaches are difficult to reach so it's hard to know what pollution is there.

In Scotland, volunteers in planes fly around the coast.

If they spot plastic pollution in the sea or on a beach, they record it and take photos.

This information can then be used to organise a clean-up.

This rubbish washed up on a beach in Scotland.

# Plastic-Free Packaging

Scientists and inventors are designing new packaging materials made from plants, seaweed and mushrooms.

They want to make packaging that will biodegrade, or rot away.

Some people make compost from food and garden waste. The compost is used to feed plants. Some types of biodegradable packaging could be put into compost.

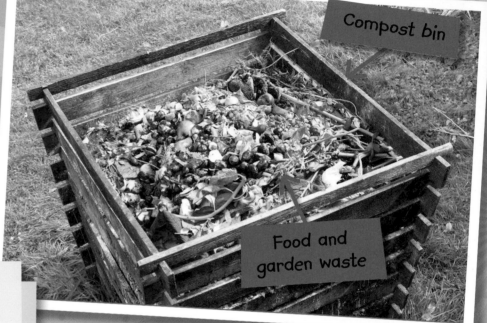

Compost bin

Food and garden waste

Compost

Scientists in Indonesia have invented packaging made from seaweed.

A farmer growing seaweed

This seaweed burger wrapper has no taste and can be eaten with the burger.

Scientists in London have invented a membrane, or skin, that can hold water.

Bags made from seaweed

It is made of seaweed and plants and can be swallowed with the water!

# Be a Plastic-Free Champion

If everyone takes small actions, it can have BIG results!

Around the world people are saying NO to single-use plastics such as straws, water bottles and plastic bags.

Never drop litter! Always recycle rubbish or put it in a bin.

Go on a litter hunt or take part in a beach clean-up with your family or friends.

Volunteers for the Washed Ashore Project in the United States clean up beaches. Then the plastic is used to make giant animal sculptures.

A shark sculpture made by Washed Ashore.

Before you buy something plastic, such as a toy, think about the end of its life. Will you be able to pass it on to a friend or give it to a charity shop?

Do one thing and ask your best friend to do it, too. You've just doubled the impact you will have!

Everyone can do something.

Let's STOP plastic pollution and save our oceans!

# Glossary

**biodegrade**
To rot away and become part of the environment.

**brittle**
Hard but easily breakable.

**chemical**
A substance that comes from nature or is made by people. Chemicals can be used to make materials such as plastic.

**current**
A movement of water in a stream, river, lake or ocean.

**degrade**
To break down or reduce in quality.

**landfill**
A place where large quantities of rubbish are buried in the ground to get rid of it.

**microplastics**
Tiny pieces of plastic that are less than 5 mm long.

**nurdles**
Tiny pellets of plastic that are the raw materials for making plastic objects.

**pollution**
Rubbish, liquids, gases or other substances that are harmful to living things and to the land, water and air.

**recycle**
To turn used, old or unwanted objects and materials into something new.

**sewers**
Large pipes that carry waste from homes and other buildings to treatment plants where the waste is made safe.

**toxic**
Poisonous.

# Index